Fall Ball
poetry in
the late-innings

poems by

Alan Harris

Finishing Line Press
Georgetown, Kentucky

Fall Ball
poetry in
the late-innings

Copyright © 2018 by Alan Harris
ISBN 978-1-63534-776-0 First Edition
All rights reserved under International and Pan-American Copyright Conventions.
No part of this book may be reproduced in any manner whatsoever without written permission from the publisher, except in the case of brief quotations embodied in critical articles and reviews.

ACKNOWLEDGMENTS

Hospice House published by *Poetry Breakfast* (2016)
Rain Out published by *Wilda Morris Poetry Challenge* (2013)
Pearls published by *Metric Conversions* (2013)
Not Today published by *Snapdragon* (2015)
Body Language published by *Pulse* (2016)
Shed published by *Gyroscope Review* (2015)
Still Driving published by *The Lake* (2015)
On the Run published by *Boston Literary Magazine* (2015)
Putting my Name on it published by *Sygyzy* (2015)
If Stephen King Wrote Poetry published by *The Lake* (2016)
Fall Ball published by *Gravel* (2016)
Waiting for Something to Happen published by *Boston Literary Magazine* (2017)
Black Smocks published by *Boston Literary Magazine* (2017)
In Between Colonoscopies published by *Panoplyzine* (2017)
Life in the Past Lane published by *Panoplyzine* (2016)
PICC-line published by *Temenos* (2016)
The Snowman and the Sun published by *Poetry Breakfast* (2016)
Memory Stick published by *Anomolie* (2014)
The Man in the Moon published by *The Tishman Review* (2015)
Go Gentle published by *Snapdragon* (2017)
Man in the Middle published by *Remembrance Anthology* (2017)
The Whisper published by *Psaltery & Lyre* (2017)
The Hard Questions published by *Spirits* (2017)
Dead Man's Hat published by *Word Fountain* (2017)
Sunrise, Sunset published by *Memoir Mixed Tapes* (2018)
Footsteps published by *Portage Magazine* (2018)
The End is Near published by *Portage Magazine* (2018)
I Can Hear the Future published by *Celestial Musings* (2018)

Publisher: Leah Maines
Editor: Christen Kincaid
Cover Art: Photographer: Jacob Pierzchala
            Photo concept: Allan I. Ross
Author Photo: Nicole Bell
Cover Design: Leah Huete

Printed in the USA on acid-free paper.
Order online: www.finishinglinepress.com
            also available on amazon.com

Author inquiries and mail orders:
Finishing Line Press
P. O. Box 1626
Georgetown, Kentucky 40324
U. S. A.

Table of Contents

Fall Ball 1
Time 2
Curiosity 3
Not Today 4
Emancipated Innocence 5
Conversations 6
Still Driving 7
The Man in the Moon 8
Paper Airplane 9
If Stephen King Wrote Poetry 10
Broken Promise 11
Shed 12
In Between Colonoscopies 13
Final Buzzer 14
Sweet Invitations 15
Moment of Clarity 16
Rain Out 17

I Can Hear the Future 21
Man in the Middle 22
On the Run 23
Three Gallons of Diesel Fuel 24
The First Dance 25
The Whisper 26
The Tree 27
Putting my Name on it 28
Body Language 29
Box of Toys 30
Falling Forward 31
Broken Hip 32
Honoring the Non-resuscitated 33
The Snowman and the Sun 34
Sunrise, Sunset 35
Full Measure 36
Let there be Dancing 38

Self-Help 41
Age Line 42
You can go now 43
Pearls 45
I Married the Coyote 46
Memory Stick 47
Cognitive Decline 49
PICC-line 50
My Vacuum Cleaner doesn't Suck like it used to 51
Life in the Past Lane 52
The Gospel of Thomas 53
Silence 54
Shallow Breathing 55
Take What I can Get 56
The Hard Questions 57
Footsteps 58
Go Gentle 59

Hospice House 63
Spirituality 64
The Gift of Young Visitors 65
I didn't see this coming 66
Victory Lane 67
Hospital Bed 68
Lost Balance 69
Corners and Curves 70
Black Smocks 71
They're talking about me 72
Burn 73
Waiting for Something to Happen 74
Amenable 76
Dead Man's Hat 77
The End is Near 78
Noli Timere 79

For
Henry "Hank" Raby
Michael Hernly (Long-haired Mike)
and Marie Woods Bohnhorst

Fall Ball

> Aging is a game we all hope to play well.

I have been a fan of the game for some time now, up in the bleachers shelling peanuts with my father long after he passed. Now I find myself in the bullpen warming up, waiting for the call.

Some of us don't even know we are on the roster. Then one day we find ourselves among friends on the DL. We notice changes in our bodies, sometimes in our minds. As a society we are not yet ready to welcome those changes. I knew something was up when I could no longer find the strike zone, when my fastball looked like a change-up, when my *high and tight* looked more like *low and away*.

Self-preservation demands that we start playing softball in the autumn of our lives. The distance to first base is a little shorter and the ball is not only bigger but we have more time to see it.

Life is a set of compromises.

Eventually we come to grips with the realization that there are no more contract extensions. Unfortunately, the world finds more value in our rookie card than it does to sit beside us on the bench. Still, it's hard to walk away from the game.

Fall Ball

The nights are cooler
as the daylight dims
in these late season opportunities
to throw the ball around
and get in a few more at-bats

That's why we squeeze in double-headers
while we're still able
to pick up a bat
to stare down the pitcher
to clear the bases one more time

And at season's end
we finally admit the truth
how our goal was never to finish first
but to look God in the eye
and be called safe at home

Time

whenever we spent time together
my grandfather never wore a watch
my father said he'd lost it

if you ask my wife
that explains why I don't wear a watch
she says I'm afraid of losing one as well

but I suspect the truth lies
somewhere in my longing
to be just like my father's father

living life without a constant reminder
of how little time
we all have left

Curiosity

On one shore of the river
are the living
casting our fishing lines out
in pure and simple
hope
while on the other shore
our ancestors
cast their lines out of curiosity
for it's not that hope is gone
over there
it's simply irrelevant
and at the end of the day
what really makes us all human
even dead ones
is the unrelenting
biological
spiritual
instinct
of curiosity
wondering what
in heaven's sake
will happen
on that day
when our lines
finally tangle

Not Today

The sand on the beach
recognizes her footsteps
as each grain moves aside
out of respect and appreciation
for her loyalty

Her gait is more cautious
than the year before
as the sea gulls pay attention
in hopes she'll spill the contents
of her picnic basket

The lifeguard tips his sunglasses
as she returns a smile
like strangers do who understand
that there are bonds
in familiarity

All the while waves
caress her feet flirtatiously
carrying messages from
Virginia Woolf
and Edna Pontellier

With pockets free of stones
yet full of stories
she smiles at the invitations
and whispers
—*Not today*

Emancipated Innocence

As spring came to an end
I locked away my inner child
at the bequest
of anticipatory adulthood

I embraced the heat of summer
with my so-called maturity
far too busy to enjoy
the warmth of the sun

It took autumn's fleeting beauty
to help me understand
my most precious seasons
are far too brief

Thankfully the winter
freed the child within me
Together we try on old mittens
and await the final snowfall

Conversations

As I listen to them in my living room
those pictures on the wall that speak to me
in a language all their own
a dialect where nouns and verbs
are replaced by memories
where syntactic rules
are governed by reflection

And there we converse
about chance and purpose
where upon I find *myself*
highly motivated
to take a few more pictures
while there's still time
to keep the conversation going

Still Driving

your odometer refuses to roll over

your coolant light is on
and there's nothing I can do about it

I keep your tires in good shape
and just had new wiper blades installed
but there's so little else I can do

your gas gauge can't be trusted
your driver's side blinker won't even wink
at the headlights up ahead
or the trooper trying to get around us

neither of us can tell if the siren's for real
or if it's the background of a song
on your AM radio

and in the rear view is either
a tow truck or a hearse

content to follow us home

The Man in the Moon

there's a bench on the moon
where my father sits
reading Byron in the shade

whistling *Amazing Grace*
smiling like the photo on the wall
whispering my mother's name

while he waits
watching the horizon
for the Earth and I to appear

until our eyes
meet
in the moonlight

where we take turns
crying in silence
until we both laugh out loud

Paper Airplane

Life is like a paper airplane
carefully designed
in hopes that our maiden voyage
will catch a breeze
and sail further than others
who have gone before us

And once fallen
it is our hope to be lifted up
to fly again
and again
until our creases are no longer sharp
our flights ever shorter

and eventually the thought
to soar once more
is unnecessary
or at the very least
no longer worth
the harsh landing

If Stephen King Wrote Poetry

it still goes on
those little things
that annoyed me about you
the casket's closed
but the kitchen cabinets remain open
it's like you're here
going through the junk drawer
leaving the toilet seat up
the dog wags its tail
at your La-Z-Boy
your favorite beer
fills my fridge
your socks lay on the floor
our grandchild
still talks to you
your aftershave
calls my name from
hand towels and pillow cases
the damn lawnmower
refuses to start without you
along with the old Ford,
barbeque grill,
and the sump pump
which leads me to
your photo on the wall
as I wonder if those eyes
are asking me to follow
or simply saying *good-bye*

Broken Promise

My father warned me
about unspoken promises
of honor and respect
of relevancy at the very least
made by naïve children

Now I listen as everyone else
has something to say
but me
in the clamor
of one-way conversations

they stop to ask
from time to time
if anyone else heard
a faint whisper
an echo in the dark

I do not let on
that the sound
they think they overheard
was something inside me
breaking

Shed

Shakespeare said we shuffle off
or at the very least shed
unmatched socks
worn-out shoes
faded suits
fit for neither weddings
nor the funeral dance

using the Bard's metaphoric
boiler-plated
bullet-pointed boxes
stacked in the cellars
stuffed with stuff
real and surreal
crowding the corners
of our basements
our foundations
clogging our attics
our minds
we check off each item
until the only mortal coil
we have left to shed
is the last breath we take
to say
sayonara, baby

In Between Colonoscopies

have you ever cleaned your house
by setting it on fire?
that was the first one at 50
the prep was as bad as I'd heard
they sent me home with color photos
of six polyps along with an invitation
to return in two years

up until then
I'd only been high-risk
for eating too much ice cream
for laughing too loud
at *The Three Stooges*
for crying when Ray Kinsella
asked his dad to play catch

after the fourth colonoscopy the polyps returned
The Three Stooges stopped being funny
I no longer saw myself as Ray
I became his dad
knowing that soon the only opportunity
to embrace second chances would have to come
through cornfields on the way back from the dead

Final Buzzer

Mother played the game in the big leagues
her lifetime stats were void of fouls, fumbles, and flags
She was a golden glove, an Angel in the outfield
who was never called off-sides
never intercepted
she overcame the rough
and always kept her stick on the ice

While never allowing the game to come to her
you could expect she would spike the ball
nail the landing
hit the green
and find the sweet spot on any bat

Her name will never appear in the Hall of Fame
but friends, fans and loved ones
will forever carry her rookie card in their hearts
for never throwing in the towel
for leaving everything on the field
and for staying in the game
long after the bleachers had cleared out

To her credit she never kept track of
runs, points, or goals
yet we will all remember
how each and every score
not only ended, but began with love

Sweet Invitations

There's laughter in the playground
faint echoes in the park
tempting me to climb the slide
one more time

At the beach
gentle tides whisper an invitation
to dive
into waters long receded

My weathered hands
hold tight to memories
reaching inside my heart
to bring me back to you

Moment of Clarity

she taught our children
reasons to watch the sky
to witness planets
separated by distance
time
return to align
like siblings
searching for the bonds of familiarity
of gravity
of love

and then one day she was gone
like the eclipse
when she taught us
not to blink
or we'd miss the celestial truth
hiding in the dark
in the corner of our eye
where epiphanies of love
grab you by the throat
in a moment of clarity

Rain Out

it rained
the day of my father's
funeral

we had tickets
to the baseball game
before it was called off

just like everything else
when death earns
a victory on the road

home from the cemetery
I watched the TV
as the grounds crew rolled out the tarp

the announcer advised
the young pitcher
to keep his rosin bag dry

soon enough he'd be
throwing fastballs down the pipe
and change-ups in their face

keep that glove oiled
senses sharp
muscles loose

and don't forget
to hold your place
in the rotation

for life
unlike death
is often rain-delayed

Storytellers

...the seventh inning stretch

I Can Hear the Future

on clear nights my mother gathered us in the backyard
as she unwrapped the sky
presents to wide-eyed children who should have been in bed

among the gifts were the moon,
Venus, Mars, Jupiter,
the Perseids on warm August nights
the Lyrids in the spring
we wore winter coats over our pajamas
for the Geminids in December

because I thought I already knew everything
I once told her that we were only looking into the past
something a teacher had told me

something about the time it takes for light to travel to our backyard
but Mom smiled
ran her fingers through my hair

and whispered that seeing the past was easy
but when searching the night skies with her children
she was able to hear the future

in the years that followed
I have often been heard saying to my own family
as we watched the night skies together

how Grandma so loved the moon
Venus, Mars, Jupiter
the Perseids on warm August nights
the Lyrids in the spring
and with an old winter coat covering her pajamas
the Geminids

and in those moments I came to understand
that my mother, in fact
had heard the future

Man in the Middle

Five of us passed up Sunday breakfast
on *The Arizona*
on our way to the 8am Mass
when the first munition detonated
but we all blamed the Marines
for Sabbath-morning maneuvers

Then the planes came in low
Japanese markings were undeniable
there was smoke
black water
sailors swimming to shore
—on fire

All five of us ran
for sanctuary
shoulder to shoulder
but a Zero swooped in
strafing the ground at our feet
until one of us fell

The man in the middle
took four bullets
one for each of us
boys became men
as we each placed a hand
upon a wound meant for us

And the man in the middle smiled
happy to be surrounded
and held onto by friends
proud to have taken their bullets
on the day he alone
reached sanctuary

On the Run

Our Indian guide
an experienced tracker
led the posse across the parking lot
hot on the trail
of an aging desperado

until they came upon
a discarded gait belt
an empty bottle of Celebrex
and a four-pronged quad-cane
with worn-down rubber tips

but there was no sign
of the outlaw on the run
who had escaped in broad daylight
unnoticed by LPNs
and CCTV cameras

they finally sent the posse home
and noted in the police report
that the suspect had avoided capture
with the help of his grandson's
awaiting El Camino

as fellow bandits and other patients
believers all in folklore and fate
share weekly whispers on Bingo Night
of how he had bided his time
for his turn to fade away

Three Gallons of Diesel Fuel

I arrived in Bearcat Base
scared and angry
at the age of 19
encouraged by the draft board
not discouraged enough by a young wife soon to cheat on me
and all in all
against what little good judgement I ever had in my youth

the whole rotten deal
stunk to high heaven
reinforced as I stepped off the chopper
the first time I set boots on the ground
and could smell what we had done
with malice and three gallons of diesel fuel

I figure it was once beautiful
but that's what we do to beauty
we defoliate
we send in tree crushers
we rape the hell out of it

until everything you see
makes you long for home
until everything you smell
makes you gag

and when you pissed-off your CO
you joined me in the mornings
with three gallons of diesel fuel

poured into each latrine
followed by a match

to cleanse our stench with fire

The First Dance

It was New Year's Eve at The Red Rail
as I entered the smoked-filled bar
and saw you there
with my friends at a round table in the back
I took the only seat left
that seemed to call for me
at the other end of the table
from your beautiful hair
from your holiday dress
from your smile
which I presumed at the time
was an invitation

Then the band started to play
and everyone headed to the dance floor
arm in arm
which was just the encouragement I needed
like a lyrical treasure map
in A-minor
with four chords calling my name
ushering me to follow the curve of the table
as it led me to you
as it led us to the floor
for the first dance
changing the future forever

The Whisper

I heard it again
last night
but no one believes me
so I've stopped talking about it
I even deny it
when they ask
am I still hearing children at the door

not children
just one voice
young
confident
familiar

whispering
through the keyhole
the same question
night after night

I never offer an answer
I suspect that's because
I'm afraid
but the child is undeterred
persistent
and quite possibly
rhetorical

asking me once more
      …is that all there is?

The Tree

I recall a tree that once stood in front of the old farmhouse
upon which I learned to climb
upon which I could see
where I came from
upon which I could dream
of my own future

One day they came to widen the road
the tree had to fall
but though I mourned its passing
I could forever smell its rich and hearty roots

And I wonder if
when my time comes to fall
to make way
for the eternal widening of roads

will my roots reach out to your senses
to whisper that I was once here
encouraging you to dream
of the future
to remind us both
of where we came from

Putting my Name on it

Years ago my brother and I
fought over everything
but he caught on quick
to the art of verbal dueling
knowing in my predictability
I would demand
that he give something up to me

"Why?" he would ask
"Because your name's not on it," I'd reply
so with a crayon
he wrote his name
on the couch
on the TV
on my favorite cereal bowl

And now that he's gone
I've put my name
on all of our
shared memories
ready for the day
that his ghost asks me
to give it up

Body Language

after my father had his stroke
we never spoke again
but that didn't stop us
from reading each other's faces

recognizing the punctuated pauses
periods and question marks
etched in eyes, sighs, and sad smiles

it took both hands to hold one of his
that first day in the hospital
as my eyes whispered how much I cared
and his smile replied, *Thank you*

but before I left his side that night
our sighs acknowledged
the painful truth

that despite how well
we finally understood each other
it became regrettably apparent
of how little time we had left to talk

Box of Toys

a poor country family once owned a horse
though we certainly could not afford
a decent lock on the stable door
and when that old black mare
went for a walk by itself
like it had a purpose
like it was time
to go away…

I'm not sure why
I keep on going back
to the day my sister and I
played together in a box of toys
father had brought from the Goodwill
that day he heard the black mare had died
unless it's because I am about to take my walk
and hope memories can substitute for toys in a box

Falling Forward

my father died at home
at the front door
after three strokes and two heart attacks

he was still on the move
and until now
I never thought about where he was going

Victor Kiam once said
that even if you fall on your face
you are moving forward

we are all moving forward
Dad taught me that
and Victor helped me see it as a good thing

I still don't know where Dad was headed
but after three strokes and two heart attacks
I know he finally got there

Broken Hip

the injured animal
stared into the headlights
of passing traffic
sitting alone
in the median
with a broken hip
watching and waiting

as people drove by
leaving behind
a momentary sigh
while life-long memories
of the night
their eyes met
followed everyone home

Honoring the Non-resuscitated

friends gathered in the dining room
of the nursing home
to share whispers and suspicions

was the old girl dead
when the nurse's aide found her
slumped over her hospital bed-rail?

it's no secret that the nursing home staff
adheres to a strict Do Not Resuscitate policy
Could she have lived another day?

would she have wanted to?
what were her dying words?
was she alone?

these are the topics that crisscross
the dining room tables
as each resident

takes their turn honoring
the latest escapee
who found her way home

The Snowman and the Sun

Despite the snowfall
or because of it
the snowman lifted himself up
from the quiet blanket
of nothingness
and said to the sun
> *This is my yard*
> *these children*
> *who made me*
> *are my responsibility*
> *I'm here to watch over them*
> *and to protect this house*

The sun, smiling
reminded the snowman
that there will come a season
when your duties will melt away
but the love that created you
will remain vigilant

Sunrise, Sunset

Listening to Roger Whitaker
crooning ballads
beats television any day
on a hospice ward

Sunrise, Sunset
    Sunrise, Sunset

in Whitaker's whistle
the songbird beckons back
to Hayworth Creek
where time drifts by without you

Sunrise, Sunset
    Sunrise

Where you swim once again
with turtles and snakes
where you splash water
in Virgene Miller's face

Sunrise, Sunset

Where your friend, Frederick
who died of pneumonia
at eight years old
teases—*you got a girlfriend*

    Sunrise

So you dive below the surface
one last time
holding your breath, holding her hand
but this time—you close your eyes

    Sunset

Full Measure

Lincoln said it at Gettysburg
of how
they gave the last full measure of devotion

Jimmy was from Boston
his dad had died
and his mother had to raise his special needs brother alone

Vietnam never called him
he was the man of the house
he could have stayed home

but Jimmy enlisted and took the higher pay rate
the combat bonus
to send home to his mother

he was stationed in Blackhorse Base Camp
drew the sympathy of commanding officers
and given a repair rig to drive

but the VC were neither sympathetic
nor knowledgeable
about US Army vehicles

the smaller faster trucks stocked with ammo
were both in front of and behind
the boy from Boston

all he was hauling were spare parts
gears, tires, a transmission
along with a commitment to send his paycheck home

Charlie hid in the field
waited until the largest vehicle lumbered by
and detonated their deadly charge

ammunition got to where it needed to go
tires and gears and transmissions
were easily replaced

but a son's love
his last full measure of devotion
lay scattered in the jungle far from Gettysburg and Boston

Let there be Dancing

on the first day
God was heard to say

    Let there be dancing

and since then
you and I have danced together
from dust to flesh and back again
all the while heartbeats and solar winds
have provided the cosmic rhythms
for kindred spirits and soul mates
to waltz to the echoes of the Big Bang
which is no bang at all
more wind really than percussion
allowing us to step to the pace
of an eternal melody filling the vacuum
a sentient vibration which understands
that without dancers
the universe would be a figment
of a non-existent God's imagination

Lucid Moments

...it's the eighth inning and there's tension in the bullpen

Self Help

Don't over-protect me
especially from myself
keep your stainless steel toilet rails
leave my throw rugs alone
I'll put on my own socks
thank you
button my own shirts
tie my own shoes
bathe myself
use the stove and do my own laundry

I'll compromise
for safety's sake
you can take either
my car keys
or my cigarettes
but not both

So if you think
you know what's best for me
out of some ill-conceived notion
then at the very least do me a favor
and leave one bullet in the chamber
of the gun I keep
under the allergy-free pillow
at the head of my
empty marital bed
complete with rubber sheets
side-rails
and an emergency
call button

Age Line

Watch as the world
pays attention
to the little things
previously excused
or ignored
like forgetfulness—a young person's idiosyncrasy

                an elder's proof of dementia

Once you cross the age line
new rules apply
a presumption of
frailty and forgetfulness
will follow forever
like a shadow in the shade
hidden but always present
waiting to label you
as substantially sub-par
dangerously defective
simply because you crossed

              ....

                an imaginary line

You Can Go Now

Near the end
you may lose the ability to speak
thanks to the morphine drip

That's when you hear it
words like fingernails
across a chalkboard

it's code for *good-bye*
they don't mean anything by it
why don't they just say…

Goodbye
or even better…
thank you

When you lost your first job
they said
you can go now

When your first marriage broke apart
you were told
you can go now

You've heard it enough
you don't need
another invitation to leave

If you could speak
you would say
I'll go when I go

Whether or not
they stay to the end
is up to them

Unless you could speak
if only to whisper
to impatient mourners

you can go now

Pearls

in the nursing home cafeteria
she wears her pearl necklace to breakfast
her fingers caressing each gem
like it was Aladdin's lamp
and as each wish is granted
she travels through time
from pearl to pearl
secretly opening doors to the past

the staff physician blames her age
falsely accusing longevity
for suspending her belief in tomorrow
and precluding any coherent
interest in today
but if only science understood
she doesn't simply
recall and remember
she returns

to call out her lover's name for the first time again
to calm her newborn's fear of the light
her toddler's fear of the dark
to caress her mother's hand for the last time once more
re-living moments that made a difference
moments that prove to her heart she was there
moments that ensure her humanity
shining forever
like pearls strung along the thread
of her life-story

I Married the Coyote

doctors inspect my husband with one eye
embracing their version of the truth
their perception limited by
the confines of a single dimension
which they define as
the *standard of care*
with no depth
no texture
simply the flatness found
in pre-Pixar animation
while he is but a '50's cartoon caricature
Wile E. Coyote in a hospital gown
to their feathered protagonistic prognosis
communication void of words
their biased outlook bolstered
by cruel imaginary lines
as everyone awaits the imaginary train
to pierce the imaginary hole
in the imaginary mountain
standing between us all

Memory Stick

I carry a memory stick
on a string
around my neck

My stick archives
one thousand images
a million words

My stick helps me
remember who I am
who you are

My stick helps me
remember the first time
my child walked, talked

the last time
my grandpa laughed,
cried

If I misplace my stick
I may forget
your name, my own

So archive my picture
on your stick, on a string
around your neck

Mention the last time
you saw me laugh,
cry

Carry me with you
until you forget
my name, your own

before your life
is but a frozen archive
on someone else's memory stick

Cognitive Decline

I took an extra moment today
to think of my child's name
and while I was mulling over
the possibilities
I saw in my mind's eye
the day she was born
relived every moment
nothing forgotten
proof that after everything else
our humanity
lives on
within the spaces
between birth and death
indisputable evidence
that we are all examples
in the miracle of life
and discrediting
the arbitrary importance
of remembering names

PICC-line

a needle inserted
into a venous cavity
built for the long haul

transporting fluids
a modern medical miracle
designed to deliver nutrients

or to steal another sample of blood
to measure the ineffectiveness
of the designer drug *du jour*

it saves poking around by amateur vampires
in hospital gowns
intent to transform me into a pin cushion

instead, they've turned me into
a number on a chart
an occupied bed

another over-medicated dreamer
tubing in the revenue stream
of tomorrow's healthcare merger

floating on a placenta
made of gel foam
and rubber sheets

wading in the darkness
waiting in the light
for the doctor

to cut the PICC-line
the umbilical cord
and send me home

My Vacuum Cleaner doesn't Suck like it used to

My doorbell's dead
the A/C's AWOL
the fridge freezes veggies
and spoils milk
the dryer doesn't dry
the mixer doesn't mix
the blender doesn't blend
I even have to micromanage the microwave

and whether I like it or not
the sink *is* sinking
along with any hope
that God's telemarketer will call
to offer my body
my life
my soul
an appliance warranty

Life in the Past Lane

cancel the MRI
stop the Aricept protocol
I'm not renewing the Namenda
it's neither dementia
nor delirium
casting my mind adrift
it's not depression
driving me back
down old roads
so what if I'm more interested
in the rear view mirror
than the road up ahead
let me return
to my comfort zone
my home sweet home
clean the wax
from your stethoscope
and listen to my soul
you might just overhear
a memory whisper
a professional courtesy
asking you politely
to back away from my chart
and allow my past
to take it from here

The Gospel of Thomas

there's something inside each of us
ticking away
like the heartbeat of a trapped soul
or the timing mechanism
of a spiritual IED

there are only so many ticks in its tock
so before your parts are parceled out
among the human dust and debris
or worse
you fade to nothing

because what you left to simmer—to boil over
scalded clean your every metaphoric fiber
memory and meaningful thought
sterilizing all proof
that you ever existed

so before it's too late
let it escape—what's inside you
to stay behind after you're gone
to remain vigilant and provide evidence
that you were once here

Silence

Silence has power
to open doors, knock down walls
kill your enemies and destroy friendships

Silence is not a virtue
it is a cloak, a black ball
a hidden dagger, a suicide vest

Silence is not golden
unless the very rich, the alchemist, the metallurgist
fashions a mausoleum door

to tempt thieves and keep out loved ones

Shallow Breathing

unbeknownst to her
she had been practicing
with every bated breath
in preparation for those
moments that determine
the full measure of life

    from beginning to end

where rhythmic measures
of shallow breaths
both spiritual
and evolutionary
usher in angels
of life and death

Take What I Can Get

I'm free to struggle
in a downhill spiral
one step closer
two steps back

where progress
cures and recoveries
hide like a liver donor
at an AA meeting

but I'll take what I can get
for soon I will sleep forever
never to wake and smile
as the morning sun says hello

The Hard Questions

The Celebrex bottle is child-proof
much to the chagrin of the children
hiding in shadows
roaming the halls

like echoes
ominous but not threatening
yet nudging her
with silent whispers

to admit that
there's no solace
in sleep
when haunted by questions

like how will she open this bottle?
what day is it?
will anyone hear
her final words?

anyone besides ghosts
regrets
and the bad memories
she shares her bed with

Footsteps

My husband heard them first
footsteps
in no apparent hurry
like someone waiting patiently
for something to happen
but then again he was one of those
poets
always looking and listening
on good days
for similes and metaphors
on bad days
irony and foreshadowing
connective tissue made of allusions

He's gone now
there's no one to listen but me
to the footsteps pacing in the hallway
on the kitchen floor
stopping to read my letters
on the dining room table
moving across the room to touch the curtains
accidently kicking the dog's dish
like a ghost with nowhere to go
like the rustling pages of a final chapter
echoing tomorrow's footsteps
of Dickinson's mourners
marching to and fro

Go gentle

I lie in a hospital bed
reading what Dylan Thomas
had cried out to his father
in what would become iconic verse
unwavering instructions
to not go gentle into that good night

and I wonder
what Dylan's father would have wanted
if only he had been asked

as for me
I will neither burn nor rave
at the end of the day
I will not rage
against the dying of light
nor the coming of darkness

for if it's all right with you
into that good night
I will gladly go gentle

Hospice Bed Confessions

…two outs in the ninth with the bases loaded

Hospice House

They've been numerically labeled
all their lives
first husbands, second wives
the last four of their social security number

not anymore—
here each room is the name of a tree
What used to be 227
is now the Magnolia Suite

Each cold metal door
replaced by natural grains
not a barrier but a metaphor
that swings both ways

Reminding us how both patient
and wood had stood tall
through thunder and rain
sunrises and sunsets

Demanding little but
water and sunshine
providing shelter, food
the very air we breathe

Giving roots and buds
broken limbs and fallen leaves
a reason to gather
for one last sunset

Spirituality

They say the closer to death we get
the closer to God we become
the hospice pastor believes so
as does the lady with the guitar
the agency sends to sit with me
on Wednesday afternoons

I'm a hard case
says the pastor
that's why, I suppose
I get serenaded with Amazing Grace
on hump days
to let go and let God

But even a hard case can be spiritual
it's just the way I see it, have always seen it
God has never been captured
not the least of which
by old men editing the narratives
of other old men

I don't know where death leads
I'm no expert…yet
just a leaf in the wind
another piece of driftwood
bobbing in the water
appreciating the ride

and now the pastor has stopped coming
because I'm a hard case
a non-believer in meetings with makers
but since I've been wrong before
leave some money in my pockets
enough to buy God a drink

The Gift of Young Visitors

when my grandson stopped by today
it brightened up the hospice floor
to have the voice of a 10-year-old
skip through the hallways

as an unwritten rule
they keep children away
making us and death
less visible to the young

but as any grandson of mine will do
he broke the rules
and demanded to tag along
to visit Grandpa

as soon as I saw him
I shouted Bingo!
I knew something good
would happen today

he wasn't sure what *Bingo* meant
as it is rarely heard
in video games
or on the playground

we came to an understanding
that an appropriate translation
from his grade school lexicon
would be *boom shakalaka*

that's the main reason
to allow children to
mingle with the dying
so much for us to learn from each other

I didn't see this coming

this isn't a bad place to be
just not what I expected
the hospice nurses have seen to my every need
it's like a two-star hotel with maid service
maybe three-star
but I didn't see this coming
I look around the room
and realize that the only way out is death

I get an idea
if I can't return to the condo with my wife
I'd like to buy a little house
back in my home town
I have the money
I just need believers, friends
and co-conspirators
willing to help me pull it off

but time fades like childhood memories
and while the nurse ups the dosage
of liquid morphine
reality whispers into the confessional
that has become my final four walls
apologizing for the little things
that cannot be
like going back home

Victory Lane

We were going to get married
in Victory Lane
before the chemo
before the admission to hospice
I was going to wear a tux
over my favorite racing shirt
—*Work Sucks, I'm Going Racing*

Victory Lane is for celebration
it's where you go
when you leave the rest behind
when you're sure there's nothing more to give
when all that remains
is to wave to the crowd
and hold the one you love

We were going to get married
in Victory Lane
before I realized we were as good as wed
before I over-heard God call my name
to celebrate in Victory Lane
I'm headed there now in my new favorite racing shirt
—*Life Sucks, I'm Going Racing*

Hospital Bed

The hospice nurse suggested it
my own bed
in the living room
with side rails
so that I won't fall on the floor
controls to raise my head
elevate my feet
a vinyl mattress cover
to protect me
from the previous patron
all the while
my wife sleeps alone
in the other room

I don't like the new sleeping arrangement
I don't like the changes it has made
in my own house
there on the door jamb
left behind by the man
who delivered the bed
is a scratch mark
that will remain long after I'm gone
along with the new sheets
my wife purchased
for the bed in our room
the one without side rails
where I will never sleep again

Lost Balance

There was a time
her hair was colored red
she had danced with the Rockettes
she once crossed the Rio Grande
before Roe v Wade
she campaigned for McGovern
she took her children to museums
she taught them to laugh
she survived cancer
a rotten marriage
only to be put on a morphine drip
to ease the pain
caused by a throw rug
left behind by the ex
upon which she had fallen
for the last time

Corners and Curves

he proudly explained to me
his lifelong philosophy
of corners and curves
it's all about decisions, he'd say
and how we come to them
or avoid them altogether

he was a man of action
rather than allow any decision
to meander along the slow cautious edge of a curve
he cut to the quick
cut to the chase
he embraced the commitment

to act now and leave nothing to chance
to get to where he was meant to be
it helped him accept where he ended up
in a hospice bed
where he anxiously awaited the opportunity
to make one more hard right

Black Smocks

I leave the door of my hospice room
open
the view from my wheelchair
intrigues
green smocks, yellow smocks, white smocks, blue smocks
black
dance back and forth with
purpose

green knows the way to the caf'
and back
yellow knows where the linens
are hidden
white oversees the so-called
vital checks
blue simply volunteers
to listen

but black's a walking reminder
death's on duty
waiting to wheel me away
upon white's order
so that yellow can
change the sheets
while green feeds and blue listens to
the next departee

They're talking about me

There they go again
talking about me
as though I'm already gone
yet remain
the topic of discussions
with everyone but me

They don't want my opinion
that would only hamper
their version of the truth
I'd only get in the way
of treatment plans
or lack there of

Because if I was engaged
in the process
the prognosis
the planning stage would not start with
how soon will we need
this bed?

Burn

start with the headboard to our bed
then move to the coffin,
my favorite suit,
the blue tie I liked so much,
drawings from the grandkids
the rose you bought
just for this occasion

burn it
burn it all
and let the smoke
enter your lungs
where our memories
will simmer
forever

Waiting for Something to Happen

There you are in the hospice bed
wondering if anyone really knows
when it all comes to an end
you thought you did but you don't
they gave you six months
that's what the referring physician
stated in writing
that's what the Medicare reimbursement
is based on

if you live any longer
whether you like it or not
you do so knowing
—number one
you've proven your doctor wrong
again
—and number two
the hospice is taking care of you
for free

Unless there is a miraculous
recovery
which never happens
your time above ground
is more limited than it was before
before the doctor got ahead of himself
before the insurance revenue stream dried up
before your friends and relatives stopped calling
because they figured you'd be gone by now

So you wait for something to happen
you up your liquid morphine
you listen to your favorite music
you touch faces in old photos
of those who can still stir memories
despite the medication
and you wonder if it all was worth it

and you wonder what's next
and you wonder if you're already gone

Amenable

I was informed that my condition
was not amenable to treatment

and as a direct result
furniture was removed from my living room

I suspect the Davenport that once belonged to my mother's mother
was not amenable to being put in storage

and if anyone is interested in my opinion
I am not amenable to sleeping alone

on a cold mechanical poor excuse for a bed
facing the television

calling out to visitors and family
to pull up the bedside commode

and join me in watching *The Walking Dead*
as long as we are all amenable

as you tell me how lucky I am
to shit, piss, and eat all in the same room

I was amenable to many things in life
how it ends—not so much

Dead Man's Hat

I found this hat in the desert
the head it belonged to was nowhere in sight
I shook out the sand, trusting
any bugs that had called it home
were thoroughly baked in the hot sun
along with the previous owner

I call it my dead man's hat
no need for fancy names
I figured one of us was headed nowhere
and the other headed somewhere else
I just wasn't sure
which one was which

Like most relationships
it started out rough
fitting snug at first
until after the chemo
where it was there for me
that's when we became inseparable

I imagine the previous owners
were ranch hands
if not gunslingers
who proudly wore it
a hundred years ago or more
though the tag says *Made in Thailand*

Which brings me to an important request
I want you to save the hat
return it to the desert
let it bake in the sun
or if you've a mind to
you're welcome to try it on

The End is Near

I remember the man
in the long beard
carrying the sign
THE END IS NEAR
I'm sure he was not as old
as I remember
though I'm optimistic
the hair on his face
most certainly was

And I asked my father
near what is the end?
what is it next to? close by?
approaching upon?

My father ignored the man
as he looked at his watch
and explained to an 8-year-old
that everything has an expiration date
including life
and only a fool
needs to read it on a sign

Noli Timere

I saw an old woman
at cash register
number five
place soup cans
and corn starch
and Raisin Bran
on the moving belt

she turned around
and told her husband
words he'd always remember
…*I forgot the broccoli*

so off he went
and upon his return
from fresh fruits and vegetables
with broccoli in hand
she laid there on the linoleum
cashed out by death's apprentice
in a grocery store smock

and until the day he died
he heard her voice echo those final words
…*I forgot the broccoli*
and he was not afraid

For over 30 years **Alan Harris** has worked with nursing home, home care and hospice patients, actively listening to the stories of their lives. Harris is a hospice volunteer who helps patients write memoirs, letters, and poetry. In 2016 he was named the Sparrow Home Hospice Volunteer of the Year. Alan returned to university later in life and earned a Masters in Creative Writing from Wayne State University in Detroit, Michigan. He is the recipient of the 2014 John Clare Poetry Prize as well as the 2015 Tompkins Poetry Award from Wayne State University for his *Fall Ball* collection. Harris is a two-time Pushcart nominee. His first chapbook of poetry entitled *Hospice Bed Conversations* from Finishing Line Press has been nominated for a Midland Author's Award.

www.ingramcontent.com/pod-product-compliance
Lightning Source LLC
Chambersburg PA
CBHW070549090426
42735CB00013B/3128